NOTES FROM THE
DIVIDED COUNTRY

NOTES FROM THE
DIVIDED COUNTRY

{ p o e m s }

SUJI KWOCK KIM

LOUISIANA STATE UNIVERSITY PRESS
Baton Rouge

2003

Copyright © 1994, 1995, 1996, 1997, 1998, 1999, 2000, 2001, 2002, 2003 by Suji Kwock Kim
Manufactured in the United States of America
First printing
Cloth
12   11   10   09   08   07   06   05   04   03
5   4   3   2   1
Paper
12   11   10   09   08   07   06   05   04   03
5   4   3   2   1

Designer: Amanda McDonald Scallan
Typeface: Sabon
Printer and binder: Thomson-Shore, Inc.

Library of Congress Cataloging-in-Publication Data:
Kim, Suji Kwock, 1968–
    Notes from the divided country : poems / Suji Kwock Kim.
        p. cm.
    ISBN 0-8071-2872-4 (alk. paper) — ISBN 0-8071-2873-2 (pbk. : alk. paper)
    1. Korean War, 1950–1953—Poetry. 2. Korean Americans—Poetry. 3. Korea—Poetry. I. Title.
    PS3611.I455N68 2003
    811′.6—dc21

                                                                    2002155402

Contact the author through the Academy of American Poets, at www.poets.org/skkim.

WINNER OF THE WALT WHITMAN AWARD FOR 2002

Sponsored by The Academy of American Poets, the Walt Whitman
Award is given annually to the winner of an open competition among
American poets who have not yet published a book of poems.

Judge for 2002: Yusef Komunyakaa

CONTENTS

ACKNOWLEDGMENTS

Grateful acknowledgment is made to the editors of journals where poems first appeared, sometimes in different form and under different titles: *Columbia:* "Nocturne"; *DoubleTake:* "Montage with Neon . . ."; *Hawaii Review:* "RICE"; *Kenyon Review:* "Borderlands," "The Chasm"; *Michigan Quarterly Review:* "The Couple Next Door"; *The Nation:* "Hanji: Notes for a Papermaker," *"Hwajŏn," "P'ansori"; New England Review:* "The Road to Skye," "Translations from the Mother Tongue"; *The New Republic:* "The Robemaker"; *Paris Review:* "The Korean Community Garden in Queens," "Monologue for an Onion"; *Ploughshares:* "Flight"; *Poetry:* "Leaving Chinatown," "Occupation"; *Salmagundi:* "Between the Wars"; *Southwest Review:* "Song of Ch'u: To the Sea-Wind"; *Tin House:* "On Sparrows"; *Yale Review:* "Looking at a Yi Dynasty Rice Bowl."

"The Couple Next Door," *"Hanji:* Notes for a Papermaker," "Montage with Neon . . ." and "Monologue for an Onion" are reprinted in *Asian-American Poetry: The Next Generation,* ed. Victoria Chang (University of Illinois Press, 2003). "Montage with Neon . . ." is reprinted in *Century of the Tiger,* ed. Frank Stewart (University of Hawaii Press, 2003). "The Korean Community Garden in Queens" is reprinted in *Imprint: A Korean American Anthology,* ed. Elaine Kim (Asian American Writers' Workshop, 2003). "Levitations" originally appeared in *MUÆ,* ed. Walter Lew (Kaya Production, 1995). "Nocturne" originally appeared in *SALON* (www.salon.com/weekly/kim.html). "Aubade Ending with Lines from the Japanese," "Levitations," "The Robemaker," and "Transit Car" also appeared in *Shankpainter,* ed. Elizabeth Arnold and Jhumpa Lahiri (Provincetown: Fine Arts Work Center, 1998).

It's an honor to thank the National Endowment for the Arts, the Fulbright Program of the IIE and Korean-American Educational Commission, the Stegner Program at Stanford University, the Fine Arts Work Center in

Provincetown, the New York Foundation for the Arts, the California Arts Council, and Washington State Artist Trust for crucial support that made the completion of this manuscript possible. Thanks to the MacDowell Colony and Yaddo, and also the Djerassi Foundation, Hedgebrook, Millay Colony for the Arts, Ragdale Foundation, Ucross Foundation, and Villa Montalvo, for residencies that offered shelter and sustenance.

For their faith and generosity over the years, I'm deeply grateful to all my friends and teachers. *Kamsahamnida* to my 17 Syllables community: Edmond Chow, Jay Dayrit, Lillian Howan, Brian Komei Dempster, Roy Kamada, Caroline Kim, and Grace Loh. For their last-minute help, special thanks to Sabina Chen, Jill D'Alessandro, Mark Doty, Carmen Einfinger, Carmen Giménez-Roselló, Antonio Lapuos Jocson, Timothy Liu, Mary Rakow, Lloyd Schwartz, Elyse Singer, Michael Tyrell, the heroic staff at LSU Press, and most of all, Edward Hirsch, Garrett Hongo, and Yusef Komunyakaa. Love, love, love to Sunja Kim Kwock, Fred Kwock, Kerry Kwock, Kim Hak-young, and everyone in my family, in every country.

{ I }

И я молчу . . . Как будто умер брат.

— Анна Ахматова, "Ива"

And I am silent . . . as though a brother had died.
—Anna Akhmatova, "Willow"

Generation

0

Once I was nothing: once we were one.

1

In the unborn world we heard the years hurtling past,
whirring like gears in a giant factory—*time time time*—

2

We heard human breathing,
thoughts coming and going like bamboo leaves hissing in wind,
doubts swarming like reconnaissance planes over forests of sleep,
we heard words murmured in love.

3

We felt naked bodies climb each other,
cleaving, cleaving,
as if they could ride each other to a country that can't be named.
We felt bedsprings creak, felt the rough sailcloth of sheets dampen,
felt wet skin hold them together and apart.
What borders did they cross? What more did they want?
Bittersweet the sweat we tasted, the swollen lips we touched, the chafe of
      separate loins:
bittersweet the wine of *one flesh* they drank and drank.

4

They called us over oceans of dream-salt,
their voices *moving over the face of the waters* like searchlights from a
    guardtower.
We hid, and refused to come out.
Their cries followed like police dogs snarling from a leash.
We ran through benzene rain, flew through clouds of jet-fuel.
We swam through hydrogen spume, scudded among stars numberless as
    sands.
We didn't want to be born we didn't want.
Blindly their hands groped for us like dragnets trawling for corpses,
blindly their hands hauled me like grappling hooks from the waves,
the foaming scalps of ghost-children laughing, seaweed-hair dripping,
the driftwood of other children who might have been.
Out of chromosomes and dust,
cells of hope, cells of history,
out of refugees running from mortar shells, immigrants driving to power
    plants in Jersey,
out of meadowsweet and oil, the chaff of unlived lives blowing endlessly,
out of wishes known and unknown they reeled me in.

5

I entered the labyrinth of mother's body.
I wandered through nerve-forests branching in every direction,
towering trees fired by feeling, crackling and smoldering.
I rowed through vein-rivers.
I splashed in lymph-creeks between islands of glands.
I leaped rib to rib, rung to rung on the spine,
I swung from the ropes of entrails.
I played on organs, leaped through a fog of sweet oxygen in the lungs.
I clambered over tectonic plates of the skull, scrambling not to fall
down the chasms between, the mind-mountains where I could see no bottom.
I peered through sockets at the brain brewing in cliffs of bone
like a gigantic volcano, with its magma of memories, magma of tomorrows,
I could have played there forever, watching, wondering at the vast expanses
     inside,
wondering at the great chambers in the heart.
What machine made me move into the womb-cave, made me
a grave of flesh, now the engine of beginning driving forwards,
cells dividing, cells dividing:

now neurons sizzling, dendrites buzzing,
now arteries tunneling tissue like tubes hooked to an IV;
now organs pumping, hammers of hunger and thirst pounding,
now sinews cleaving, tendons lashing meat to bone:
meanwhile my skeleton welding, scalp cementing like mortar,
meanwhile my face soldered on, hardening like a mask of molten steel,
meanwhile my blood churning like a furnace of wanting,
meanwhile my heart ticking like a bomb—*is-was, is-was:*
then cold metal tongs clamped my forehead and temples,
then forceps plucked me from mother's body like fruit torn from a tree:
then I heard a cry of pain—mine? not mine?—
then a scalpel's *snip snip* against the umbilical cord, like razors scraping a
     leather strop:
soon I felt sticky with blood and matted fur, surgical lights blinding,
soon I felt tears burning my skin—*Why are you crying? Why am I?*—
I didn't know who or what I was, only that I was,
each question answered by the echo of my voice alone: I, I, I.

The Tree of Unknowing

Uncertainty, take me into the forest
leaf by leaf—

where an immigrant sits in a Jersey slum,
a young mother rocking her child.

Where, along the endless road, are you going away from me like a
      cloud?
Like a cloud, like a cloud?

I lay in your arms, watching your lips.
I touched your chin with my tiny fingers.

Your loneliness sang to me,
each word a crumb of light, burning in the skull—

until a galaxy of sparks flashed among the branches,
lighting the way where?

I lifted my head. What was it I saw
in your gaze, the maze

of you: corridors of years, corridors of war, black wheat-hair
      ripening—
the last shape sown in closing eyes.

The words have their own woods.
Where the words can't go further: where the woods begin

that make us mad, too real and not
real enough. Whose memory was it? Why did I feel such joy?

Look, the cloud-tree will never die—

I wonder who you were: I wonder
because you were.

The Tree of Knowledge

Fact explains nothing. On the contrary, it is fact that requires explanation.
—MARILYNNE ROBINSON, *Housekeeping*

1

Go back, you'll never see it again—
the loved face without shadows, the loved face rushing forward to the
hospital
not knowing what will happen, knowing nothing.

I'm two. Walking unsteadily, like a drunk dwarf.
Step by step you're learning *what flesh is heir to,*
you're learning what cleaves:

no angels watching over us, no flaming sword guarding the gates of para-
dise,
only the tree branching in every direction, dividing leaf from leaf
life from life—

know: no: you are you: not
I: this is Admitting: not the Waiting Room: not the ward
where our mother's hooked to a machine for blood—

each name a nail,
something driving the world into words,
something engraving the body into a sentence that can't be ungrieved.

I ripped her womb being born.
For weeks she bled so much she asked the doctor what it meant.
—*Nothing Bleeding is normal after delivery It'll stop.*

Why didn't he listen to her?
Unchecked the lacerations never healed properly.
Unstitched the uterine tissue jagged and scarred, scarred and shrank.

Shrank too small to hold my brother,
trapped inside:
still feeding him, still breeding and breeding him with no room to grow,

driving his skull harder against womb-walls the larger he became,
making his torso swell and cramp his limbs until they stunted,
feet kicking fists pounding in terror,

mouth smothered eyes crushed
because there was nowhere to go,
because there's no other world to enter.

When they plucked him out with forceps, they say he cried beyond belief.
How long had he been suffering, before anyone knew?
Was the worst over?

So wept we, so much did it cost us to enter this life
wound in a mortal shroud of body, alone,
one.

2

Why couldn't the doctors account for it?
Nothing in the ultrasounds.
Nothing in the amniocentesis.

Noting intrauterine growth retardation.
Noting severe mental and physical disabilities.
Of unknown origin.

3

Have you ever hurt your heart wanting, wanting for years,
asking why what happened
happened, hoping beyond the last desire to feel hope—

Father and mother ordering round after round
of bloodwork, tissue biopsies, chromosomal tests
(six years passing)—

And the child-I-was,
wandering the dusty halls of the clinic crammed with immigrants waiting
(migrant workers, refugees, war orphans like my father?)—

wondering why they laughed, or wept
strange tears that frightened her—forest of countless faces leaving—
What would you have done? What was the right thing to do?

4

The way he looked at her afterward, sleeping in a blue hospital gown,
the way she slowly opened her eyes and saw—what?—in his face,
can't be spoken:

how she covered her face and cried *No*,
how the screams echoed in the room re-echoing in my skull never to die,
how a doctor in a white coat told me to wait outside,

now the girl-I-was leaving, turning in the doorway,
now a nurse staring then glancing away, pretending not to notice,
now other nurses bustling past, used to worse,

here carrying vials,
here pills or syringes for sedation,
here trays of scalpels and sharp metal instruments,

somewhere a surgeon scouring his hands in a steel sink,
somewhere an orderly pushing a machine glittering with wires,
somewhere my sister clamped inside an incubator, weighing three pounds,
    almost nothing:

no one knowing if she'd live,
no one knowing why she should be one too, *retard, fool,*
no one knowing why the child-she-might-have-become would never be
    born.

Why wasn't once enough?
What makes us and makes us begin, blocking the way back,
what drives us out *into the four corners of the known world?*

I can still hear the scrape of hinges as the door swung shut,
hear the cries muffled by wood,
dissolving, coil by coil, as I walked forward:

recoiling from shouts of other patients, footsteps, shrieks of children scur-
    rying past,
interns in blue-green scrubs hurrying to mothers in labor,
to deliver infants born, never to be unborn:

I can still smell rubbing alcohol and sick-sweat in the corridor,
taste ammonia,
see dirt on the floor, see cinderblock walls, see the brown water-stained
    ceiling,

feel the buzzing of fluorescent lights above,
feel the clattering of gurneys and IVs on wheels below
like the rattling of chains:

stupid I, *subject,* taking it in, taking it all in,
seed by seed, never to be unsown, cells dividing, limbs ripening—
breeding what? what for?

I can't stop remembering, recalling to the last splinter
the window sill with its knots,
the rough husk of peeled paint in my hand

as I held on, looking outside
at the parking lot, the toll-booth, the exit to the freeway,
bodies driving forwards forwards forwards—

What does it mean, one way only
one life only?
Why was mother hospitalized so long?

It was midsummer then, all the elms in gold-green leaf.
She was younger than I am now.
She could never bear another child.

5

She never says she blames me, but I'm to blame.
How did I know what I know?
From husks of things unspoken, things unspeakable,

from kneeling between wood pews knuckles whitening,
from coins crammed into a tithing box prayers stammered again and again,
from words tasting of gnawed nails, spit, ash—

Lord, how long wilt thou hide thy face?
Why should we be patient, when death lies at the end like the fruit of life?
Why didst thou bring me forth from the womb?

Seek and ye shall
seek: I wanted to die, but death
is no remedy for having been born.

I don't want to go on,
counting, recounting the aftermath
like an eye forced open, hideously seeing and seeing and seeing—

sweet fruit of the brain shriveled in its rind of skull,
face twisted limbs wasted,
one ear withered to a worm, one eye soldered shut—

after what happened branched off from what might have happened,
each leaf and its shadow cleaving, each *is* and *is-not* mocking the other
like good and evil: but which is which?

Out of the womb of nothing, out of the infinite
grave of other lives, other worlds,
I see the shadow I could have been, the man and woman you might have
    become:

and caught inside each, a stillborn soul, *infans,* with its tongue torn out.
I'll never know them.
I want to pursue them. I want them to break free.

O ghost-brother, ghost-sister. Silence like nothing
but not nothing. Dream-vowel. Implacable O.
Lie to me. Say you forgive me for being born.

Middle Kingdom

Gruel, crumbs on a table
of ice, a labyrinth of snow:
and infinite distances
in the small box of the kitchen.

Mother chopped pieces
of her heart into the skillet.
Brother and I heard oil sizzle
until we huddled in shame.

She salted the meat with tears.
She cried if we ate
and cried if we refused to eat,
warning *You'll go hungry.*

Each morning her heart grew back.
Each evening father went away—where?—
while she cleaned room after room
not knowing when he'd come home.

What was the rest of their story?
Between them lay silences,
secrets lost in the hissing woods
of happiness and unhappiness.

Giant ghosts haunted the halls,
father-mother, sister-brother
dwarfed by our other selves,
dwarfed by who we never became.

Mother prayed every night—for what?
Brother couldn't speak, but spoke
by beating his skull against the floor.
I hated the words that never broke

whatever spell bound our house:
but when she caught my eyes open
I shut them and bowed my head,
pretending to say grace, pretending to pray,

so as not to frighten her.

Translations from the Mother Tongue

for my mother

1. Khimjahng

It held you once. Chora of hands splashing water,
to scour and peel mugwort piled in bamboo creels.
Chora of knives hacking sowthistle or lotus root,
steel beating against wood boards, blades glinting.

It was. Now November sun slants into your eye
from a foreign sky. You scrub, rinse, chop, wring.
In America you labor through *khimjahng* alone—
without your sisters, an ocean away, or your mother,

long dead. There must be hunger in these rhythms,
if not happiness. To cut and crisp cabbage with salt,
to smear shreds of wild radish, bracken or scallion
with chili, skinned anchovies, garlic crushed to pith.

Next your arms work the spices in. Slap. Slur.
Nose stinging from onion-juice and pepper-fumes,
eyes tearing. Your fingers slowly blister, stain.
Meanwhile your mouth waters, starved for the taste

of home, not wanting to wait until winter seasons
what you bury now. Pack the clay crocks well;
cram the *khimchee* jars with what will sour and scald.
This is the covenant of autumn, its hard blessing:

what survives cannot survive unscathed, not fallen
burr or shoot, not fists of spore or snarled taproot.
Dig the furrows deep, sow the *hahngari* in rot.
Steep them in the element that destroys and saves.

2. P'ansori

You are singing of bamboo flutes and barrel drums,
clapping as your village celebrates the birth of a child,

red peppers spread out on straw mats to dry.
You sing of hemp-weavers spinning fabric for *hanboks,*
knife-grinders, papermakers pounding mulberry bark,
workers hauling burlap sacks of pinenut or quince.
Fishermen watch mask-dances set to *kayagum* and gong.
Street peddlers hawk *makkolli, soju,* soup boiled with sea-bracken,
shark fins, dried squid, ginseng roots pickling in jars, tiger balm.
There are sweet rice-cakes and pears piled like sandbags,
and paper lanterns lit with candles for the wounded,
sculling down the river to the open sea.
There are soldiers in your song, gunfire, a city bombed to rubble,
and starved dogs gnawing the bodies of the dead.
A surf of objects that beat against the doors of the skull
and are never abandoned,
the sand-grain variousness of things that can't be owned
or forgotten, of people who have vanished.

I listen for your mother in your voice and cannot know
if I find her. Not much lives on, from one generation
to the next. Not much, but not
nothing: maybe the Paektu mountain tune
you both loved, crags grizzled with pine, rock maple,
black walnut, their burred and scabrous spines.
Shagbark or needledust. Gingkos scoured by snow.
Or cabbage chopped and scummed with pepper,
stocked in clay vessels, rocked into the soil like seeds.
Buried in fall, dug up in spring, soured, spiced,
to nourish and to burn. Tell me if this is true.
I want to know what survives, what's handed down
from mother to daughter, if anything is,
bond I cannot cut away, that keeps apart what it lashes together.
And I want to know what cannot be handed down, the part of you
that's only you, lonely fist of sinew and blood,
deep in your gut where cords lash bone, nerve, breath,
the part of you that first began to sing.

{ II }

Es soll in seinum Spiel durchaus ersichtlich sein, daß »er schon am An-
fang und in der Mitte das Ende weiß« . . . ist es die primitivste Art der
Einfühlung, wenn der Schauspieler nur fragt: wie wäre ich, wenn mir dies
und das passierte?
—BERTOLT BRECHT, »Kleines Organon für das Theater«

It should be apparent all through his performance that "even at the
start and in the middle he knows how it ends". . . it is the crudest form of
empathy when the actor simply asks: what should I be like, if this or that
were to happen to me?
—"A Short Organum for the Theatre," trans. JOHN WILLETT

Occupation

The soldiers
are hard at work
building a house.
They hammer
bodies into the earth
like nails,
they paint the walls
with blood.
Inside the doors
stay shut, locked
as eyes of stone.
Inside the stairs
feel slippery,
all flights go down.
There is no floor:
only a roof,
where ash is falling—
dark snow,
human snow,
thickly, mutely
falling.
Come, they say.
This house will
last forever.
You must occupy it.
And you, and you—
And you, and you—
Come, they say.
There is room
for everyone.

Borderlands

for my grandmother

Crush my eyes, bitter grapes:
wring out the wine of seeing.

We tried to escape across the frozen Yalu, to Ch'ientao or Harbin.
I saw the Japanese soldiers shoot:

I saw men and women from our village blown to hieroglyphs of viscera,
engraving nothing.

River of never.
River the opposite of Lethe,

dividing those who lived from those who were killed:
why did I survive?

I wondered at each body with its separate skin, its separate suffering.
My childhood friend lay on the boot-blackened ice:

I touched his face with disbelief,
I tried to hold his hand but he snatched it away, as if he were ashamed of
    dying,

eye grown large with everything it saw, everyone who disappeared:
pupil of suffering.

Lonely O, blank of an eye
rolled back into its socket,

I was afraid to see you:
last thoughts, last dreams crawling through his skull like worms.

Hwajŏn
[Fire-field]

There is no need to keep
humiliating me: even you must feel
these stubble-fields have been slashed enough,
crags glinting blackly like sockets
burned bare, blood-glitter of mud,
wind driving across the torn, steaming soils.
But you cannot know
what it is to be trapped inside the dirt
without a voice, thirsty roots
thrusting toward air, shoving above
rock-rung and gorse—; nor can you feel
this ore tearing through
its throat of stone, erupting from soil-silence
like the moment my voice first
hurls me, astonished and stinging, into the acid light.

(During the Japanese occupation of Korea, rural home-
lessness rose drastically and peasants were forced into
slash-and-burn farming in the mountains.)

Resistance

for my great-grandparents

1

Snuff out the collaborators, sense by sense:
the eye that caught a Japanese soldier beating you,

a man who looked like your brother,
as like you as you were to yourself:

the nose that smelled gunmetal and sweat:
the tongue I bit until I tasted blood:

the skin shivering, each hair standing on end
to feel you flinch at every blow.

Cut off the ear that heard our children scream for mercy,
that heard bone crack when he broke your jaw with a rifle-butt.

What was worse, his beating you
or your seeing them see you beaten, humiliating you beyond reason,

ashamed this might be how they'd remember you,
afraid their cries would kill us all.

I whispered *Lie quietly. The worst will be over soon.*
And calmed myself to keep our children calm.

He took you away to prison.
You lived behind watchtowers and barbed wire for the next sixteen years.

2

Bless the chestnut trees I climbed as a boy,
the fields of dragon-tongue fern and manchurian windflower I ran through.

Bless the old men smoking gourd-leaves in bamboo pipes
thinking "anti-Imperial thoughts,"

bless the children playing *yut* during school,
expelled for not swearing the loyalty oath to the Emperor.

Bless the deported who refused to pray to the Empire's gods,
to bow down before sun-colored *torii* gates of Shinto shrines:

bless the exiles who ran opium from Burma,
who hawked sesame oil or fried chicken-claws in Shanghai.

Praise the prisoners arrested for speaking Korean,
for not answering to Yamada or Ichida or Sakamaki, their new names by law:

praise the guerillas who starved during the '29 uprisings,
"hunger mountain" before the barley ripened.

Remember the coal miners ordered to war in Manchuria,
the Land of the Rising Sun's "East Asian Co-Prosperity Sphere":

remember the factory workers who joined the resistance in Vladivostok,
relocated at gunpoint by Stalin in '37 to Kazakhstan.

Remember the "Comfort Corps" raped forty times a day,
the woman screaming who could not scream because she was on fire.

In Cholla-namdo we used to break the bones of corpses' feet
so their souls wouldn't walk back from the other world, but would you walk
    back?

Once the guards forced us to watch a comrade being skinned alive.
Later they bludgeoned prisoners to death to save bullets.

What won't we do to each other?
After liberation I saw a frenzy of reprisals against former collaborators.

An old man—guilty or innocent?—lashed to a grille of barbed wire. Bodies hung from trees on the sides of the road, swaying.

At night a sickle glinted in the sky, sharp and pure. What did it reap. Summer wind sang through the corpse-forest.

Animal Farm, or
Song of the Colonial Governor-General

Admit it. You hate the body
because it can be broken,
stabbed, shot full of holes.
And so you became a butcher.

Say the spirit cannot be broken.
Say you see better than anyone
how fiercely an ox, a hog, a cock
fights to stay alive, until the end.

You wonder how nothing seems
to stop this rat: sucking, gnawing
through cement walls to snatch
scraps of gristle—not knowing

what you need to kill, or why.
Beat it with a shovel: skin-slither,
pestle of skull and will. Admit
it shamed you to cover with dung.

The Chasm
(August, 1950)

In the dream vultures circle above my mother's cousin.
Eye the gash blown in his belly

by Soviet T-34 tanks or U.S. rocket-launchers
shooting at each other blind across the Naktong River—

a million refugees caught in the crossfire,
crossing far as the eye can see.

Vultures smell the kill.
My mother screams when one drops

on his chest, thrashing for foothold,
his small body shaking beneath its wings,

talons ripping away strips
of flesh like bandages.

She beats it with her walking stick
until it flies hissing to another corpse.

Then another one lands, then another, then another,
her beating the stick until they fly away too,

not for good, swarming again and again to his half-gnawed body,
wave after wave.

Her mother shouts at her to *leave him*.
Digs her nails into her arm and drags her on.

My mother can't see his face anymore
for their jaws, chewing on twisted entrails,

insides pulled out like ropes unlashed from the mast of the spine,
all the bleeding sinews and nerves, strange jellies,

all the hieroglyphs of generation.
Why won't they speak.

———————

I know you were real, even if I can only see you
in dreams, I see

we'll never meet.
It's humiliating to wake up

alive, fifty years later, when I couldn't have saved you.
I couldn't have saved a dog.

For the birds change their faces
and wear the faces of soldiers.

Song of Ch'u: To the Sea-Wind

for Hwang Tong-gyu

Now I'm frightened. I see
only the inside of things.

Chartless this dark.
Waterskin seared away

by gasoline, bile-black
brine shot with fire—

and a sea within the sea
boiling with scalp-rags,

viscera, crumbs of skull.
Gulls cry, starving.

Cut in gullet and gut.
Severed from me: but not

enough. I cannot forget
I cannot help them.

Wind, where is the wall
between looking and feeling

lashed—wall that will keep
their hunger from mine,

incinerating eye that is
no eye, that cannot weep?

Wind, blow within.
Burn away my eyes to blank

and bone: scald my tongue
until it's skinned to nothing. I am kin

to you already. I want
to be one.

Fragments of the Forgotten War

for my father

You whom I could not protect,

                     whose suffering I'll never know,

when will I forget you:
when will I forget the NKPA soldiers who took you away for questioning,
so we never saw you again?

We three sons fled south in January 1951

                         without you, with a million others
on Shinjangno, the old Imperial Highway between P'yongyang and Seoul—
oxcarts crammed with blankets and crying children,

                         whips lashing mules,
old men bent double hauling straw mats on *chiges* roped to their backs,
mothers carrying *pojagi*-swathed bundles on their heads.

I felt artillery crash miles away in the soles of my feet, the ground shuddering.
I heard the drone and snarl of engines as fighter-planes swarmed toward us
like a war in heaven but not heaven,

                     a war between gods who weren't gods,
B-29 bombers strafing "to subject

                     suspected Red guerrillas to free-fire"—

now missiles whistling on their search-and-destroy,
now the endless columns of refugees screaming in terror,
now delayed-fuse demolition bombs exploding all around us,
blowing craters larger than houses,

                     firing white phosphorus flares 3000 feet high,
while we knelt like beggars before the blasts,

                     using the dead as shields, corpse-greaved,
covering our faces from the blizzard of shrapnel,
blizzard of limbs and flaming skin,

                     of all who left this world in a grave of smoke.

I'll never forget the smell of burning flesh.
I'll never forget the stench of open sores, pus, gangrene,
                    the smell of people rotting who hadn't died yet:

or the cries of the wounded moaning without morphine,
a boy sinking his teeth into his arm
                    to take his mind off the gash that ripped his stomach,
biting down and down until you saw bone glinting through
                                        like teeth in a mass grave.

At night we fought for the few standing barns, shacks, outhouses.
Without fuel we burned dung for heat
                    until the light from our fires drew bombers.
We caught fever and frostbite from walking hundreds of miles
through mud and snow,
                    walking through Taejon, the Chollas, Taegu, Chinju.
When food ran out we ate cattle feed,
                    ate bark, ate lice from our own bodies
until our gums bled,
                    until we could only shit water by the time we got to Pusan.

What I wouldn't give to bring back that miserable village I hated as a boy.

Sometimes in my dreams you hoot like a soul-owl,
What have you done with your life,
who will you become, who, who, who?

I can only speak to you in broken things,
I can only speak in bullets, grenade-shards, mortar casings and broken ROKA
    barricades:

I know I'm orphaned,
I know you suffered, but I'll never know how.

I think of the loneliness of the dying,

                  the bodies I saw along the way, rotting separately:

I think of that boy biting his arm

                        who didn't live through the night,
wild dogs gnawing at his skull in the morning, his whole face an "exit wound":

I think of a carcass foaming with maggots, the bone black with hatching flies.

Flight

We ran from a home

                              we never saw again.

Saw nothing

                                 remain ours.

My arm shot

                    from my body. My wife's broken

neck. Our son burned

                       into a wing of smoke.

A peeled face boiling with flies.

                              A man tearing

his gangrened leg off

                  with his hands. A girl with her eyes

blown away. She was still

                                screaming.

I know you

                              cannot help us.

We will die before you

                              are born.

Things flee

                              their names—

Ash. Bone-salt. Charred embers

                              of skull

The soot is

                              mute.

Looking at a Yi Dynasty Rice Bowl

after So Chongju

Seeing this plain
white clay—

white laundry slung
on a line in my lot.

Rough hemp,
shirt and trousers

I must leave
unfolded forever.

Like my brother taken
north during the war,

clothes hanging
like a brother

who will never
come back,

I am finally ready
to have as they are—

Montage with Neon, Bok Choi, Gasoline, Lovers & Strangers

None of the streets here has a name,
but if I'm lost
tonight I'm happy to be lost.

Ten million lanterns light the Seoul avenues
for Buddha's Birthday,
ten million red blue green silver gold moons

burning far as the eye can see in every direction
& beyond,
"one for every spirit,"

voltage sizzling socket to socket
as thought does,
firing & firing the soul.

Lashed by wind, flying up like helium balloons
or hanging still
depending on weather,

they turn each road into an earthly River of Heaven
doubling & reversing
the river above,

though not made of much:
colored paper, glue, a few wires,
a constellation of poor facts.

I can't help feeling giddy.
I'm drunk on neon, drunk on air,
drunk on seeing what was made

almost from nothing: if anything's here
it was built
out of ash, out of the skull-rubble of war,

the city rising brick by brick
like a shared dream,
every bridge & pylon & girder & spar a miracle,

when half a century ago
there was nothing
but shrapnel, broken mortar-casings, corpses,

the War Memorial in Itaewon counting
MORE THAN 3 MILLION DEAD, OR MISSING—
still missed by the living, still loved beyond reason,

monument to the fact
no one can hurt you, no one kill you
like your own people.

I'll never understand it.
I wonder about others I see on the sidewalks,
each soul fathomless—

strikers & scabs walking through Kwanghwamoon
or "Gate of Transformation by Light,"
riot police rapping nightsticks against plexiglass shields,

hawkers haggling over cellphones or silk shirts,
shaking dirt from *chamae* & bok choi,
chanting price after price,

fishermen cleaning tubs of cuttlefish & squid,
stripping copper carp,
lifting eels or green turtles dripping from tanks,

vendors setting up *pojangmachas*
to cook charred silkworms, broiled sparrows,
frying sesame leaves & mung-bean pancakes,

hanyak peddlers calling out names of cures
for sickness or love—
crushed bees, snake bile, ground deer antler, chrysanthemum root,

the grocer who calls me "daughter" because I look like her,
for she has long since left home,
bus drivers hurtling past in a blast of diesel-fumes,

dispatchers shouting the names of stations,
lovers so tender with each other
I hold my breath,

men with hair the color of scallion root
playing *paduk,* or Go,
old enough to have stolen overcoats & shoes from corpses,

whose spirits could not be broken,
whose every breath seems to say:
after things turned to their worst, we began again,

but may you never see what we saw,
may you never do what we've done,
may you never remember & may you never forget.

{ III }

Ciegamente reclama duración el alma arbitraria
cuando . . . otros serán (y son) tu immortalidad en la tierra.
   —JORGE LUIS BORGES, "Inscripción en Cualquier Sepulcro"

Blindly the willful soul asks for length of days
when . . . others will be (and are) your immortality on earth.
   — "Inscription on Any Tomb," trans. W. S. MERWIN

Hanji: Notes for a Papermaker

for Liu Yoon-Young

Shaped like a slab of granite
marking a grave, but light,
airy as "spirit-sheaves" lashed
from bloodroot or star-thistle,

this sheet is not for burial
but making and making of:
a broth of splinters boiled to pith,
cast then clotted to blank.

I touch it, feeling grit and slub
silk, rough as braille. Is it
enough, is this how you hoped
to earn a living, making absence

palpable as pulp, though you laugh,
seeing I'm shocked at how much work
it took. Sow and mulch mulberry.
Slash the trunks down a year later—

chopping slant to sun so stumps
regrow—when their wood's still
tender but strong enough to keep,
no worms gnawing fleam or burl.

Soak, hack the black bark off,
tilt your knife at a sharp angle
to shave the green underskin
without cutting away grain.

Scald the peeled rods with cotton-ash
so acid softens gnurl and knot.
Pound for hours until they're ground
to shreds, skeins of unlikely thread.

You show me your blistered hands.
Poor hands. When you strike a match

to fire, I almost feel the skin sting,
kerosene flaming *yontan*-coal.

I don't know what it costs you to love
this work. More than sulfur fumes
tasting of slag, flintsparks cracking,
engine-shunt as your cauldron simmers

hollyhock root to solder all
the elements in a strange solution,
an ecstasy, flecks shapeshifting,
hissing milk, spit, quicksilver.

While it smolders you drag
slung mold and bamboo grille,
sieving with steady arms, long strokes
so fiber won't snarl at the heart.

You wring water, strip your grid,
letting grume clot to the hue
of skull-rot. It'll bleach in sun
to snow, tusk-tallow, peroxide—

depending how long it's left out,
on weather—or you'll dye it
with beets, indigo, sweet potato,
all the colors you have in mind.

In my mind you've become stern.
"For what you want to be, nothing
is something from another slant,
a slate, a plot to engrave spirit

in flesh, mirror or window or O.
Now you know how hard the labor is.
If your words aren't worth
my work, keep your mouth shut."

Leaving Chinatown

Peeling a mango to share between us, your mother
laughs at the grinning fool I've become, pours me
more and more wine. You're working late uptown.
Green *platanos* searing in oil, saffron rice boiling,

black beans simmer with *sofrito,* chili, red onion
until steam clouds the room, tasting of sea-salt.
What's between us thin as mist, raveling, unraveling,
as strange. How real is it? When she takes my face

in her hands as if she would slice open a fruit,
her ravaged voice cutting through me, I see her as she
must have been once, afraid of nothing—long before

she fell in love with your father, a man who shattered
what he touched, who left her eyes galled by all the other
faces, even yours, she might have looked into with love.

Aubade Ending with Lines from the Japanese

The sound of wind hissing through muslin curtains
wakes you from a nightmare of childhood—

parents shouting at each other, someone smashing a whiskey bottle
on someone's skull, a door slamming

for good. As if you never escaped that house:
as if you weren't free.

Outside the sun slanting through palm trees
dazzles, hurts, with the painful sweetness of things that can be loved

only once: not so much that time passes,
but that love does, passing *into* me, the way light would

if it could glitter through drifting hair and seep into the brain beneath
to stain it in a way both of and beyond

myself, until it burns away what I was, what I meant
to become. My eye is peeled.

Facing the music, if it is music *(Did you mean
what you said? What will you do next? Is it too late?)*

I know I'll never know another home,
fumes of jasmine, ripgut-brome rifting our dreams of happiness

and our real happiness, the one we didn't mean
to feel, and may or may not recognize in time.

The autumn wind is blowing;
we're alive and can see each other, you and I.

Nocturne

1

If these are not the nights of empty hands,
if these are not the nights of dreams galloping
like gasoline fire over blue tar,
I wish you could see what I see
when I look at you,
wish I could give you the country
in my skull, invisible
as the horizon I followed to your eyes—
an ocean mounting within, the foam
and drone of bile-black waters washing us closer
and farther apart, always both at once,
murmur of umber, bloodwings beating in bone.

2

You cannot see waves breaking against welted shoals,
but in the rocking of our chair, maybe you hear
the hissing of the sea, biting acetylene,
or cries of tern and gull. Maybe you hear
the uncaged waters gasping against hasp and hull,
bracken churning, scalps flensed from brine.
In your shirt's rustling, I hear sailcloth in wind,
ropes lashed and pulling against the mast.
In our chair's rasp against pine boards, I hear
the creak of oarlocks, a broken scull scraping against keel.
I hear spume soaking a bowsprit crisped with salt,
as I rock into your torso, my human shore.

3

Come nearer, nearer,
for I want to see what you see—
Light a lighthouse over these broken spars,
dress me in burlap and tackle,
play on a streel of eelgrass plucked from the troughs of the sea;
charm me with bladderwrack and sole, comfort me

with a severed branch of coral, a fistful of wet wings;
sing to me of splintered driftwood and rockweed, nights full of sulfur
    foam;
lead me through the narcotic dark to a bed
of coats, your stubbled face grazing my throat,
for I want to lie with your eyelids touching my lips when I sleep,
I want to feel the bones of your silence pressing against my own.

4

I cannot see what you see, but I will paint you
a world in green, the color you most love:
I will weave you a pillow of aloe and flowering lime,
cut you a bed of wild ginger, *casuarina* and bamboo;
I will make you a city where you may dance
on bridges and rooftops of air, where you may hear
green wind blowing across green water.
Because I can't know how long the shore we make together
will hold, let me lie against you
before the waves we are wash us from each other's arms,
before that stopless tide returns,
when we'll feel the indifference of the sea.

Drunk Metaphysics

after Ko Un

I've never been one soul.
Sixty trillion cells stagger
zigzag down the street,
laughing, trash-talking, quarreling,
singing-crying, living-dying.
Sixty trillion cells—all drunk!

The Road to Skye

Is paved with sheep shit, among other things:
sandstone gravel, glinting where the asphalt
scrapes away; tufts of peat, root-rot, scum.
What the odd Highland or Cheviot woolbag
drags in with its hooves, from slough or ditch.

We laugh when we turn onto the Shiel Bridge.
More sheep. *Baa.* They Who Shall Not Want
blink, ignore the car horn honking at them,
clod off. We drive. Our flint-pocked byway
twists up a granite tor, sheering to crags below.

What is it you hoped to see, on the other side?
Blown slant from sea, particular to the smallest
sting of salt, there are instead these smells you love—
reek of abandoned shells and creels and rotted fish.
Keels greased with diesel or slime, barnacled hulls.

Looking across the Sound of Sleat you catch
terns skirling, swarming above blue fishing-boats.
Westward a gull flies across a flood of broken gold.
Shoals. Brine scalded by sun to blood and molten
steel. Colors, you say, that burn into the heart—

falling silent now until our eyes meet near shore.
I would take this road over and over, every part,
if I could see you true. Let other roads cut through
scarp or brae or wind-scathed moor, twisting
to horizons invisible in mist. Let other travelers,
who want and want and want, drive to no end.

The Couple Next Door

tend their yard every weekend,
when they paint or straighten
the purple fencepickets canting
each other at the edge of their lot,

hammering them down into soil
to stand. How long will they stay
put? My neighbors mend their gate,
hinges rusted to blood-colored dust,

then weave gold party-lights with
orange lobster-nets & blue buoys
along the planks. So much to see
& not see again, each chore undone

before they know it. I love how
faithfully they work their garden
all year, scumbling dried eelgrass
in fall, raking away mulch in spring.

Today the older one, Pat, plants
weeds ripped from a cranberry bog.
Sassafras & pickerel, black locust
& meadowsweet, wild sarsaparilla,

checkerberry, starflower. Will they
take root here? Meanwhile Chris waters
seeds sown months ago. Furrows
of kale, snapbean, scallion break

the surface, greedy for life. Muskrose
& lilac cast their last shadows. Is it
seeing or sun that makes them flicker,
as if they've vanished? They shake

like a letter in someone's hand.
Here come the guys from Whorfs
("Whores") Court, walking their dog
—also in drag—to the dunes.

I miss seeing Disorient Express
(a.k.a. Cheng, out of drag) walk by,
in tulle & sequins the exact shade
of bok choi. He must have survived

things no one can name, to name only
KS, pneumocystis, aplastic anemia.
I remember he walked off his gurney
when the ambulance came, then broke

his nurse's fingers in the hospital
when he tried to change his IV line,
wanting to live without meds. Zovirax,
Ativan, leucovorin? I don't know.

My neighbors pack down the loose dirt.
I'll never know what threads hold
our lives together. They kiss, then fall
on the grass. I should look away but don't.

Monologue for an Onion

I don't mean to make you cry.
I mean nothing, but this has not kept you
From peeling away my body, layer by layer,

The tears clouding your eyes as the table fills
With husks, cut flesh, all the debris of pursuit.
Poor deluded human: you seek my heart.

Hunt all you want. Beneath each skin of mine
Lies another skin: I am pure onion—pure union
Of outside and in, surface and secret core.

Look at you, chopping and weeping. Idiot.
Is this the way you go through life, your mind
A stopless knife, driven by your fantasy of truth,

Of lasting union—slashing away skin after skin
From things, ruin and tears your only signs
Of progress? Enough is enough.

You must not grieve that the world is glimpsed
Through veils. How else can it be seen?
How will you rip away the veil of the eye, the veil

That you are, you who want to grasp the heart
Of things, hungry to know where meaning
Lies. Taste what you hold in your hands: onion-juice,

Yellow peels, my stinging shreds. You are the one
In pieces. Whatever you meant to love, in meaning to
You changed yourself: you are not who you are,

Your soul cut moment to moment by a blade
Of fresh desire, the ground sown with abandoned skins.
And at your inmost circle, what? A core that is

Not one. Poor fool, you are divided at the heart,
Lost in its maze of chambers, blood, and love,
A heart that will one day beat you to death.

{ IV }

There is no mystery in things, but there is a mystery *of* things. . . . They are incomprehensible; not because they are such and such, but because they are.

—CLÉMENT ROSSET, "Reality and the Unthinkable"

相看兩不厭
只有敬亭山

-- 李白

We sit together, the mountain and me,
until only the mountain remains.

—LI PO, trans. DAVID HINTON

Prelude for Grains of Sand

Beyond the harbor with its tackle and roped masts,
beyond the coastal shelf's lampshells and bladderwrack,
where beds of mussels clack,
where barnacles and wentletrap crack the green hooks,
where cockle and quahog drift through dulse,
sea whip, urchin, blood star,
you sang to me, angel of unknowing, angel of nothing,
you sang me beyond song.

On Sparrows

1

You are the song that lies beyond the ear.
Nothing gnaws like you. Wing-thrash. Bloodbeat.
      A mockery of air.

Here among woodrot and dung,
I hear sparrows churring beyond the creosote-soaked fence,
beyond the dump guttered with toxins and tar,
      beyond my eye.

They are not
what is not. If they cannot
lead me to you, they carry me
beyond myself—a faint whistling
whirring through locust roots, their far-off trills
thrumming through loam and scum, three low-pitched calls
gristling through husks, bark scabbed with moss or mold.
Shreds of unbodied voice bleed off the wind—
      sweet, sweet, sweet.

Now I am afraid
my listening will erase all that is
not you. How to stay faithful
to earth, how to keep from betraying
its music—each note soaking bracken and thorn,
now burring mulch and scurf, each chur growing louder
as the birds fly closer, across a barbed-wire lot in sodium light,
across the slop-gorged pit where sewers pour,
until a swarm of bodies scatters through the sky like shrapnel, exploding
      into sight.

2

Are not two sparrows sold for a farthing?
And one will not fall to the ground without your Father.
      (King James Bible)

2

Without your Father's will.

(New Oxford Bible)

3

In the air

but not of it.

At dawn I glimpse them, simmering

like flies above a corpse-dark field.

Tinder for the eye—

black forms grating

my glance, each shape scraping

sclera and nerve like a match,

until the sparrows become

themselves.

Sunrise strikes

the horizon's strip of fuel—

until earth

ignites, the visible world spreading

like a spark thrown into gasoline

and leaping into fire.

———————

Now each steel-streaked sparrow

arrows toward me

in a whistling arc.

Bullet without a gunner.

Aircrack. Forethirst.

Of smoke and umber wings.

Their flock a blur

of blades, a shattered

grid, shreds ripping farther apart

as the birds come closer.

Now they light

                on a leafless oak,

filling its arms

                with coal-and-ochre leaves.

Now I feel my eye

                tear. I want to know what they can't

—————

resemble, these birds, what my retina

                retains

of their bodies. What is burned

                into the gaze's maze of nerves,

and what

                is changed?

I want to hold them. I see

                I will never hold them unharmed.

Now something leaps across

                each synapse intact,

to fire

                the engine of dreaming within.

And something is broken down,

                consumed in its furnace

of wish

                and will.

4

There's a special providence in the fall of a sparrow.
                (Hamlet)

4

My thoughts are lesions in my brain. I want to be a machine.
                (Hamletmachine)

5

One sparrow catches
                    my eye.
Crown
        the hues of charred iron and mud,
plump head jerking back and forth after it perches.
I love the way it never soars
                            too far from earth.
Nor does it land
                for long, scudding from branch
to lichen-crusted branch, each one
                            a temporary ground.
I love how this sparrow appears
                        to have no love
for the vertical—how it skitters across thicket and scrub,
or away,
            to flit up or down.
No grid of thought seems
                        seared into its brain,
freeing it to fly without aim but not without
pleasure, claws ungrasping the limb it leaps from,
bough snapping back with the sound of meat hooks creaking
when smoked slabs, scabbed with salt, are unhung.
O flight and joy, this ancient dance of flesh and wind,
the sparrow's bloodwinged body beating through the air—
and yet, if seen only with the eye,
not much, a machine of meat and bone,
dirt-colored, small, stricken with lice.

6

CLAY-COLORED SPARROW. *Spizella pallida* 5¼" (13 cm) A pale sparrow of
    midcontinent; plain-breasted. Note the cream crown stripe and
    sharply outlined brown ear patch.
VOICE: 3 or 4 beats: *bzzz bzzz bzzz.* Unbirdlike.

6

SWAMP. SAVANNAH. SEASIDE. FIELD.
LARK. GRASSHOPPER. FOX. AMERICAN TREE.
WHITE-THROATED. GOLD-CROWNED. VESPER. SONG.

Fugue for Eye and Vanishing Point

Give me the clarity, the sharpness
of a season when things are plainly
themselves. No smear of dreaming on the dirt.
Let my eye see without seeking more
than what's there, and find what is
is sweet. Bleach-fumes. Urine. Cement.
Bus-exhaust. Oil glittering on pistons.
Soiled needles wrapped in butcher paper.
Infinite engine trapped in skin.

Skins

Pretend I can't see
the lady in pearls mistaking me
for the kitchen help I could have been, or be.

Pretend I can't see
the busboy still working at seventy
bend over painfully.

Pretend I can't see
the maitre d'
pretending not to see.

"Dare you see a Soul—at the White Heat?"
"Anger: anger's my meat."
"So I did sit and eat."

Transit Car

(BETWEEN "ASSEMBLY CENTER," SAN BRUNO, CALIFORNIA,
AND "RELOCATION CENTER," POSTON, ARIZONA)
for Keiko Yamada

Thunder of wheels on tracks. Hidden pistons punch
and hiss. Soon a shriek of sparks, the train's iron
scrape and drag. Where she stands, 50 years in the past,

I can't hear the blast from her freight-car's arrival
crack, rifling through tags snapping from her lapel:
NAME—NUMBER—DESTINATION. Unanswerable

loyalty tests answered by internment guards.
In the blank: "Security Risk." Her skin: "Colored."
The transit car seen from within: steel bars,

a peeling windowframe, each flake-edge of paint
exact, exacting. Zinc-sheath. Chalk-husk. Snuffed.
Beneath, she sees the wood's surface has turned

to underskin, its grain stained unevenly,
hues pooling in pock and welt, gnurl and knot.
She looks at her other travelers, wanting to peer

beneath veneers of sweat and soot, clothes reeking
of kerosene and lye. Beneath. Where hope
must lie. One by one, the stations fill without her.

TULE LAKE—MANZANAR—HEART MOUNTAIN.
The plot of her attention forced to relocate again
and again, passing arrowroot, cholla, tumbleweed . . .

Face pressed against glass. Her gaze almost burning
through the wall of the photograph to meet mine.
Or am I deceiving myself? Now her glance moves

past me, past watchtowers, barracks, tearing through
horizons of barbed-wire, tearing through cinderblock
and cement. What is she looking for, staring so hard

her gaze seems to rip the lids of her eyes?
If her hoping has no edges. No skin.
Only clarity remains and it is not enough.

Levitations

Today I saw my dead great-aunt levitating over the Hudson in red sneakers and a shroud. She floated between a vodka-jello wrestling team from New Jersey and a phalanx of blond midget hookers, swinging their tiny hips.

"O, the sorrows of exile," she howled to me, the shroud ballooning around her like a parachute. Her face had started to rot. Her body was scorched and blistered as if she had traveled a long distance, over many burning cities.

"You think it's easy being dead?" she snapped, flapping her charred arms. "Especially in America?" She flared what was left of her nostrils in disgust. "Americans don't know what war *is* anymore! They think it's a TV show that happens to other people." Her lips moved vehemently, but now no sound came out of her mouth, like a Kung Fu movie with bad dubbing.

What did it mean, her coming here as her own voodoo doll? It seemed only a matter of time before I could find the right needles to pierce her back to life, as to pain!

As for the hookers and vodka-jello-wrestlers, they were all naked, except for the human-faced masks they kept trying to tear off.

RICE,
or
Song of Orientalamentations

Now.

I
see
you
completely.
I
see
the
Oriental
between
your
thighs.
Say
"boss-san."
Lie.
Beneath
me.
Stay—
I
will.
Have
you.
Still.
A
part:
a
gain:
again.
Chink-
eye—
coin-
cunt—
tit-

tit—
tongue.
Feed
me.
Make
me.
Feel.
Fill
me.
Never.
Fail
me,

thing.

Between the Wars

("Woman with Her Throat Cut," Alberto Giacometti)

You cannot hear her.
See how she lies
        beneath you, body wound
through space: as if flesh were a wound

        to space, to be stripped away
in peels of scalp, nerve,
        bone, cry.
The cast-iron is cruel, erasing

        nearly all signs of the human.
But something passes through
        the fire, the oven's mouth—
a charred head hurtling back

        as if into the past,
an arm flinching until its hand withers
        into a beast's jagged claw.
Just enough survives

        to return your gaze: otherwise
the metal breasts would not bulge
        like breasts, and the gash
where her throat rips open

        would not bleed
an almost human silence . . .
        Listen. Something stirs,
uncoils. Caul-slither. A rustle of icy,

        invisible wings—
and clawing through breath
        that is not there,
a scream wants to be heard,

wants to be born
in the ear at the heart's heart.
              Its teeth gnaw at me.
Her blood feels fresh; her body still

              writhes, sealed
in a gunmetal finish, forever frozen
              at the moment
that unseen knife cuts through—.

              Outside it is 1932:
"nothing solid, nothing durable."
              Why should this endure.
Why legs twisted around a spine,

              mocking the shape of lasting
suffering. What was I meant
              to see, why will she never
speak. This is beyond nakedness.

              I'm afraid of her cry.
I hear the sharp scalps of other waters
              foaming on no shore:
a cold wave of nothing, and nothing.

              What is it comes back
to find a voice, to unseal
              the world within the word—
unspeakable, its icy space opening.

The Robemaker
(Yi dynasty court robe)

You begin. In your arms, unreeling bolts
of silk, ramie, rain-of-silver brocade.
There is no pattern: your needle pierces

the twill blindly, eye streaming thread.
Stitch by stitch you listen
until they seam and knot. First: a field of foaming gold—

light simmering across the warp, bodied
as quince, bloodroot, muskmelon vine.
Wild-plum trees unfold their flowering arms,

spilling wine gossamers, husk-fumes, fruit—
Naked each leaf enters its garden of flesh.
And from the frame's edge, jade tigers leap

furiously onto velvet bracken, each shade
cleaving to its body. They must have
starved for this. Now they crouch and jump higher,

springing from branch to moss-burred branch,
dancing in green ecstasy. They do not want
more. Why should this hurt you, who dream

of flesh like theirs: skin that will never bleed
or gall, cloth that cannot be
ripped from the last nakedness you will come to—

stripped, and shivering, wound in a tearing
shroud of anger and desire: *more life. More life.*
The leap from light to flesh is miraculous.
Here your hand has long since moved away.

The Korean Community Garden in Queens

In the vacant lot nobody else wanted to rebuild,
dirt scumbled for years with syringes and dead
weed-husks, tire-shreds and smashed beer bottles,
the first green shoots of spring spike through—

bullbrier, redroot, pokeweed, sowthistle,
an uprising of grasses whose only weapons are themselves.
Blades slit through scurf. Spear-tips spit dust
as if thrust from the other side. They spar and glint.

How far will they climb, grappling for light?
Inside I see coils of fern-bracken called *kosari,*
bellflower cuts named *toraji* in the old country.
Knuckles of ginger and mugwort dig upward,

shoving through mulched soil until they break
the surface. Planted by immigrants they survive,
like their gardeners, ripped from their native
plot. What is it that they want, driving and driving

toward a foreign sky? How not to mind the end
we'll come to. I imagine the garden underground,
where gingko and ailanthus grub cement rubble.
They tunnel slag for foothold. Wring crumbs of rot

for water. Of shadows, seeds foresung as *Tree
of Heaven* and *Silver Apricot* in ancient Mandarin,
their roots tangle now with plum or weeping willow,
their branches mingling with tamarack or oak.

I love how nothing in these furrows grows unsnarled,
nothing stays unscathed. How last year's fallen stalks,
withered to pith, cleave to this year's crocus bulbs,
each infant knot burred with bits of garbage or tar.

Fist to fist with tulips, iris, selving and unselving
glads, they work their metamorphoses in loam
pocked with rust-flints, splinters of rodent-skull—
a ground so mixed, so various that everything

seems born of what it's not. Who wouldn't want
to flower like this? How strangely they become
themselves, this gnarl of azaleas and roses-of-Sharon,
native to both countries, blooming as if drunk

with blossoming. Green buds suck and bulge.
Stem-nubs thicken. Sepals swell and crack their cauls.
Lately every time I walk down this street to look
through the fence, I'm surprised by something new.

Yesterday hydrangea and chrysanthemums burst
their calyxes, corolla-skins blistering into welts.
Today jonquils slit blue shoots from their sheaths.
Tomorrow day lilies and asters will flame petals,

each incandescent color unlike: sulfur, blood, ice,
coral, fire-gold, violet the hue of shaman robes—
every flower with its unique glint or slant, faithful
to each particular. All things lit by what they neighbor

but are not, each tint flaring without a human soul,
without human rage at its passing. In the summer
there will be scallions, mung beans, black sesame,
muskmelons, to be harvested into buckets and sold

at market. How do they live without wanting to live
forever? May I, and their gardeners in the old world,
who kill for warring dreams and warring heavens,
who stop at nothing, see life and paradise as one.

Notes

I

The phrases *time time time* and *is-was, is-was* in "Generation" alter lines from Vallejo's *Trilce*. Besides reported speech, other italicized phrases in this section adapt quotes from the Bible, Korean folk songs, Montaigne, and *Hamlet*.

Words in "Translations from the Mother Tongue" can be glossed as: *khimjahng*, *khimchee*-making; *khimchee*, spicy pickled cabbage; *hahngari*, clay jars; *p'ansori*, story-singing; *hanbok*, silk or hemp clothing; *kayagum*, plucked zither; *makkolli* and *soju*, liquors made from rice.

II

"Resistance" is based on the writings of my maternal great-grandfather, Kim Yoon-Kyung, linguistics scholar and co-founder of the Korean Language Society (*Hosŏnŏ Hakhoe*), who was imprisoned by the Japanese Colonial Governor-General for several years during the last phase of their occupation (1910–1945). There is a small statue of him on the campus of Yonsei University in Seoul.

"Comfort Corps" refers to the estimated 200,000 women of Korean, Chinese, Filipino, Dutch, and other descent who were mobilized into prison camps for sexual assault by the Japanese Army. NKPA stands for North Korean People's Army; ROKA stands for Republic of Korea Army.

"Song of Ch'u: To the Sea-Wind" takes half its title from a poem by Hwang Tong-gyu. Poems after So Chongju, and Ko Un alter their originals. I'm indebted to the translations of Peter Lee and David McCann especially, and also Brother Anthony of Taizé, Wolhee Choe, Young-Moo Kim, Walter Lew, and Richard Rutt.

Words in "Montage with Neon . . ." can be glossed as: *chamae*, yellow melon; *hanyak*, herbal medicine; *pojangmacha*, portable roadside bar/restaurant.

III

"Aubade Ending with Lines from the Japanese" quotes Masaoka Shiki, translated by R. H. Blyth in *Haiku* (Tokyo: Hokuseido, 1949–52).

IV

The last tercet of "Skins" riffs off Dickinson, *Coriolanus,* and George Herbert, respectively.

The lines "See how she lies/beneath you" in "Between the Wars" refer to Giacometti's stipulation that the sculpture be installed on the floor so the viewer must look down on it from above. "Nothing solid, nothing durable" quotes the Guggenheim Museum catalog *Picasso and the Age of Iron.*

The robe in "The Robemaker" is imagined, although some details can be found in the National Museum at Kyongbok Palace in Seoul, the Victoria and Albert Museum in London, and elsewhere. Likewise, "The Korean Community Garden in Queens" is imagined, although some details can be found in community gardens in Astoria, Flushing, and other neighborhoods.